MW01689367

CORNERSTONES
for

Money Management

Stephen Konowalow
Community College of Southern Nevada

Allyn and Bacon
Boston · London · Toronto · Sydney · Tokyo · Singapore

ACKNOWLEDGMENTS

To my very special parents, Terry and Julius:

Thank you for teaching me how to grow and for showing me how to be energetic, persevering, focused, hard working, and persistent.

Your memory will live on in your children and grandchildren and they will pass your legacy on to their children.

To my wife Kathy and my children Rhonda, Erika, Robert and Terry:

Thank you for your love, devotion and support. You made it possible for me to accept the long and many hours it took to complete this book. Without each of you my endeavor to complete this text would not have been achieved.

A Viacom Company
160 Gould Street
Needham Heights, Massachusetts 02194

Internet: www.abacon.com
America Online: keyword: College Online

ISBN 0-205-26691-6

Printed in the United States of America

10 9 8 7 6 5 4 3 2 1 01 00 99 98 97 96

TABLE OF CONTENTS

Cornerstones for Money Management

Cornerstones for Money Management:
College and Beyond

Something To Think About: *What this book has for you.*

Many years ago, when I was about 6 years old, I remember my mother telling me a story about my grandfather and a disturbance in the old barn. My grandparents were chicken raisers and egg producers. On the farm, there was an old storage barn. One morning my grandparents and my mother were in the barn and noticed a small bird flapping wildly under the rafters, searching for a way out through the roof. Occasionally, it would land on the loft beams to rest, but then it would fly up into the rafters again, searching in vain for a way out. Each time the bird rested on the loft beams, it was closer to freedom, because the only possible escape route was to fly down through the open barn doors. Yet each time the bird resumed its search, it would fly up toward the peak of the roof and away from freedom and survival.

According to my mother, my grandfather climbed up into the loft and tried to help the bird get out. However, each time he got close to the bird, it would fly up and away from him. After half an hour of futile attempts to rescue it, they all gave up.

They left, but also left the barn door open. The bird was forgotten. A few weeks later my mother found the little bird dead on the barn floor. Not a very happy ending.

Why do I tell this story? I tell it because it gave me the foundation of my life. My mother told me this little story to make me aware of the value of being willing to change behavior. I think she wanted me to understand that when a pattern of behavior—a choice—does not work one way, it is time to think of other ways.

The bird did not survive because it failed to recognize that a new way was needed for survival. The escape and survival pattern it was applying was no longer appropriate in these new surroundings.

Birds are instinctual creatures and fly up when in danger. In fact, that has been a recognized pattern for safety and survival for birds for eons. How does one tell a bird, who instinctually knows to fly up for safety, that today safety is found by flying down? Being a creature of instinct, the bird did not have the power of choice. It could not recognize that in its new environment it was required to fly down to solve its problem. Thus, a response which had proven effective in providing survival of its species, had helped in causing the death of this one bird. The bird was not able to reason and recognize that new conditions require change and new choices.

Fortunately, human beings *can* change and *can* make new choices. Had the bird been endowed with a human capacity for creative response, it might have considered:

> "My usual pattern has been unsuccessful. I notice that this environment is different. Therefore, I will suspend my usual judgement and develop a range of alternatives to consider and test. I will even consider the obviously ridiculous possibility of flying down instead of up."

This book opens you up to new ways of thinking about **money**. It encourages open-mindedness, getting away from the familiar, seeing new patterns and possibilities, recognizing habitual/tried responses and self-imposed limitations, being willing to try something different, and having an awareness of the fact that you may be deceiving yourself regarding how you keep and manage your **money**. This book encourages you to suspend prejudgement and to explore new response strategies to increase your ability to adapt to change. It forces you to look at behaviors which are no longer functional and enables you to restructure your view to recognize and test out new possibilities. This book will help you become aware of your thoughts and your dreams.

INTRODUCTION

Are you aware that in addition to being fun, dreaming is psychologically healthy? Think for a second about your thoughts. Do you think about graduating from college? Having a family? A career? Children? A new or larger home? Living to old age? Money? Wealth? Retirement? Financial success?

Whether or not you realize it, your thoughts are dreams. And making your dreams come true—especially your financial dreams—will require effort, study, work, persistence and patience. Are you willing to put in what it takes?

What are you willing to do to make certain that you will have a secure financial plan and future?

____

____

____

____

____

____

Are you willing to put in the effort, work, study, patience and persistence?________________

When you hear the word "money," what thoughts, pictures, or ideas come to mind? Take a few minutes to complete the "At This Moment..." exercise that follows. (Note: Before making a check mark on the exercise, photocopy it so you can share it with others. In fact, before you do any of the exercises in this book, please make multiple copies of each so you can redo them and practice them over again. As you work in the area of financial management you will notice that your plans will continue to change, so multiple copies will come in handy.)

"AT THIS MOMENT. . ."

Place check marks in the spaces beside those entries which best represent your thoughts about money.

Money Is . . .

_____ not important to me.

_____ a means of security.

_____ something to spend, share and give away.

_____ very difficult to get.

_____ very difficult to keep.

_____ a measure of one's worth in the world.
_____ a way of impressing and/or proving myself to others.
_____ the root of all evil.
_____ not a pleasant subject to talk about.
_____ a means of buying freedom.
_____ hard to manage.
_____ a way of feeling superior to others.
_____ a measure of social rank.
_____ something I have to earn for it to be of value.
_____ hot stuff; it burns holes in my pockets.
_____ a means of buying love.
_____ something I try not to think about.
_____ something I need more of.
_____ insurance for the future.

So, what were your answers? Do you think that money is the "root of all evil," or "something I can never have enough of," or "something that burns a hole in my pocket," or "something to spend, share or give away"? There is no right or wrong idea when it comes to thinking about money. However, your financial success in life will depend upon your ability to manage it, save it and invest it.

GET A COLLEGE EDUCATION

Begin now to ***like*** education. You may not believe this, but one of your best investments is attending college. Do not miss your classes or take fail to advantage of your books and professors. Not taking advantage of what is available to you in college is like throwing money away. You paid for these resources. Use them!

If you are to earn a middle or higher income salary in today's economy, it is mandatory that you complete high school—***at an absolute minimum***. Think about this: if you are to earn a comfortable retirement, you will need to complete at least a community college or technical college degree. Recognize that as the country and the world become more technological, the minimum requirement for employment will be more education.

According to the **Bureau of the Census, OUTCOME OF EDUCATION, 1995** two-year college graduates earn $425,000 more in their working lifetime than high school graduates — or $10,000 - $15,000 per year. Is this difference a substantial one to you? Could you use some of that additional money to put away monthly in an investment fund? Take a look at the following chart and study it carefully.

CHART SHOWING CAPITAL GROWTH AS A RESULT OF MAKING $10,000 LUMP SUM YEAR INVESTMENTS

Annual Rate of Return	5 Years	10 Years	20 Years	30 Years	40 Years
8%	$14,693	$21,589	$46,610	$100,627	$217,245
10%	$16,105	$25,937	$67,275	$174,494	$452,493
12%	$17,623	$31,058	$96,463	$299,599	$930,510
14%	$19,254	$37,072	$137,435	$509,502	$1,888,835

Remember, the $10,000 we are discussing here is the approximate ***annual*** difference in your income if you have a two-year degree rather than merely a high school education. Recognize, too, that a four-year college or university graduate earns $700,000 + more in their lifetime more than a high school graduate—or a $15,000 - $20,000 per year difference.

Take a look at the following chart. It represents the combined median yearly income of male and female workers 25 years old and above by level of schooling for the years 1991/1992. The second column takes this same group and projects their minimum possible income for 2021/2022 using only a 3% inflation figure. Promotions, raises, and bonuses have not been considered for any group. The only comparison is by educational level.

COMBINED MEDIAN ANNUAL INCOME OF YEAR-ROUND FULL-TIME WORKERS (MEN AND WOMEN) 25 YEARS OLD AND OVER, BY LEVEL OF SCHOOL FOR 1991/1992 PROJECTED TO 2021/2022 (USING A 3% INFLATION FIGURE)

Educational Attainment	Census Bureau Calculations 1991/1992 Yearly Median Income		Projected 2021/2022 Yearly Median Income	
	Monthly	**Yearly**	**Monthly**	**Yearly**
Less than 9th Grade	1,253	15,034	3,041	36,491
9th to 12th grade (no diploma)	1,498	17,970	3,635	43,617
High school graduate (or equivalency)	1,926	23,109	4,674	56,092
Some college, no degree	2,275	27,304	5,523	66,274
Associate degree	2,475	29,484	5,964	71,565
Bachelor's degree	2,954	35,446	7,170	86,036
Master's degree	3,557	42,687	8,634	103,613
Doctor's degree	4,256	51,075	10,331	123,972
Professional degree	5,073	60,875	12,313	147,760

SOURCE: U.S. Department of Commerce, Bureau of the Census, *Current Population Reports,* Series P-60, No. 184, *Money Income of Households, Families, and Persons in the United States, 1992.*
(Data for this table was taken from material prepared February 1994.)
Material for this table was found in OUTCOME OF EDUCATION, 1995.

Notice how the previous chart illustrates the value of staying in school and graduating. A 25-year-old person with only a high school diploma will have a medium income of $23,109. On the other hand, the same age individual with an associate degree can earn a yearly income of $29,484. Stay in college/university for two more years and earn your bachelor's degree and your median income increases to $35,446. In thirty years, with a minimum inflationary increase of only 3%, the high school graduate can only expect $56,092, the associate degree holder will receive $71,565 (more than a $15,000 per year difference), and the bachelor's degree holder can expect a medium income of $86,036 (almost a $20,000 per year difference).

The message is clear: college is an investment in your future.

ONE MINUTE JOURNAL EXERCISE

A) In 30 seconds or less, jot down three major ideas you learned from this section.

____

____

____

____

____

B) In 30 seconds or less, jot down how you see yourself applying these ideas.

____

____

____

____

____

FINDING HIDDEN MONEY SOURCES

To be monetarily successful will require you to be flexible and open to change. Are you willing to make this commitment? To have money for tomorrow will require you to plan, save, shop sensibly, and invest wisely. Most of your investment capital will come from money you already have. Surprised? Do not get trapped into thinking that you need a second or third income to be able set aside money for financial independence. It is much easier than that. Most people do not realize that they already have the means at their fingertips. It depends upon how wisely and cleverly you spend and invest your money.

Are you aware that there is *hidden* money all around you? The cornerstone to financial independence is being willing to change behavior and to try something new. Try to avoid allowing old behaviors to guide you when it comes to effective money management. Unlike the bird, in my grandparents' barn, you *do* have the power of choice. You have the opportunity to use this power to find the hidden money sources. Don't let this power to get away.

WATCH OUT FOR HOUSEHOLD INCOME ENTICERS

Most people's financial problems stem from spending more money than they have. The simplest way to solve this is to spend less. Of course, that's easier said than done.

Begin now to take note of those things you purchase that you think you need but really don't. How much money is wasted on unnecessary purchases? By changing your buying habits, you could use those funds for savings and investment in your education.

Snacking. Many students spend $20 or more a week on unnecessary food purchases. How many bags of chips, bottles of Coke, candy bars and cookies do you buy each week? Okay, so you are suffering from the "munchies." Take responsibility for what those "munchies" are costing you.

I'll admit it. I, too, have been guilty of wasteful spending and used to have a three-Coke-a-day craving. I've cut it down to one Coke a day. However, when I was buying three Cokes a day, I was spending unnecessarily $3.00 or more a day. If I only bought one bag of chips or a package of cookies a day (and it was often more than that), that added another $1.00. Four dollars a day; $20 a week; $80 each month. If I took that $80 each month and saved/invested it in a fund paying 10% or more interest, at the end of 40 years I would have more than $500,000 set aside. I would not only be financially richer, but also thinner and healthier by not eating the junk food!

So, you don't want to eliminate junk food completely from your diet? Then plan ahead. Instead of buying your snacks in a vending machine, go to the grocery store once a week and buy them in bulk. You'll save 75% of what you spend buying them from a machine or over-the-counter.

Grocery Shopping. Of course, the grocery store can be a source of bad spending as well. One major tip: **Never go to the grocery store hungry.** People have a tendency to buy more when they are hungry. Also, they usually buy foods they really do not need. So, go shopping only after you have eaten. Follow your shopping list and only buy those items that are on your list. Buying impulsively can become very expensive.

The activities that follow will take some leg work, but comparative grocery store checking on your part can result in a savings of more than $100 per month or more. Could you do anything with an extra $100 each month?

EXERCISE

Discover which of the many grocery markets in your area are the least expensive. Do the comparative shopping exercise on the following pages. The results you obtain from this exercise could amount to some very large savings for you.

The exercise on the pages 7-14 will take a full 30 days to complete. You may wish to do this with a group of four or five other students. Each student will be assigned to gather data from a different grocery store. Then you will put your results together on a final tally sheet that will allow you to compare the prices at different markets and the days these prices are changed. Remember: you must decide what items you will be researching at each store.

What did you notice from doing this exercise? My own observation is that there may be as much as a 10 or 15% difference between some of the major grocery chains. I have also noted that some chains change their prices on different days of the week (that is, they raise them on certain days and lower them on others). When you did your research, did you notice whether the prices of the products you were checking varied from one day to another? Check to see which days of the month featured higher prices, which days were lower and which didn't have any changes at all. Again, in my own observations, I have noticed as much as a 5 or 10% difference on certain days of the month.

"So, what about coupons?," you ask. Whenever you shop use coupons — but be careful. Some grocery chains accept coupons and will even double or triple their face value, ***but*** their products are more expensive to begin with. Again, checking the prices regularly will help you determine where to use your coupons.

NAME ______________________________ DATE ______________________________

WEEK 1—IDENTIFICATION OF GROCERY STORES STUDIED—WEEK 1

A) ______________________________ B) ______________________________

C) ______________________________ D) ______________________________

E) ______________________________

28 DAY COMPARATIVE GROCERY STORE EXERCISE																																			
DAY																																			
DATE																																			
THE STORE	A	B	C	D	E	A	B	C	D	E	A	B	C	D	E	A	B	C	D	E	A	B	C	D	E	A	B	C	D	E	A	B	C	D	E
GROCERY ITEMS																																			
BEVERAGE																																			
COFFEE																																			
TEA																																			
MILK																																			
CEREAL																																			
1																																			
2																																			
3																																			
FREEZER																																			
1																																			
2																																			
3																																			
FREEZER-MISC																																			
1																																			
2																																			
THE STORE	A	B	C	D	E	A	B	C	D	E	A	B	C	D	E	A	B	C	D	E	A	B	C	D	E	A	B	C	D	E	A	B	C	D	E

WEEK 1

SIDE 2—CONTINUED

28 DAY COMPARATIVE GROCERY STORE EXERCISE																																			
DAY																																			
DATE																																			
THE STORE	A	B	C	D	E	A	B	C	D	E	A	B	C	D	E	A	B	C	D	E	A	B	C	D	E	A	B	C	D	E	A	B	C	D	E
GROCERY ITEMS																																			
DAIRY PRODUCTS																																			
1																																			
2																																			
LAUNDRY STUFF																																			
1																																			
2																																			
3																																			
PAPER PRODUCTS																																			
1																																			
2																																			
3																																			
DESSERTS																																			
1																																			
2																																			
3																																			
OTHER																																			
1																																			
2																																			
THE STORE	A	B	C	D	E	A	B	C	D	E	A	B	C	D	E	A	B	C	D	E	A	B	C	D	E	A	B	C	D	E	A	B	C	D	E

NAME ______________________ DATE ______________________

WEEK 2—IDENTIFICATION OF GROCERY STORES STUDIED—WEEK 2

A) ______________________ B) ______________________

C) ______________________ D) ______________________

E) ______________________

28 DAY COMPARATIVE GROCERY STORE EXERCISE																																			
DAY																																			
DATE																																			
THE STORE	A	B	C	D	E	A	B	C	D	E	A	B	C	D	E	A	B	C	D	E	A	B	C	D	E	A	B	C	D	E	A	B	C	D	E
GROCERY ITEMS																																			
BEVERAGE																																			
COFFEE																																			
TEA																																			
MILK																																			
CEREAL																																			
1																																			
2																																			
3																																			
FREEZER																																			
1																																			
2																																			
3																																			
FREEZER-MISC																																			
1																																			
2																																			
THE STORE	A	B	C	D	E	A	B	C	D	E	A	B	C	D	E	A	B	C	D	E	A	B	C	D	E	A	B	C	D	E	A	B	C	D	E

WEEK 2

SIDE 2—CONTINUED

28 DAY COMPARATIVE GROCERY STORE EXERCISE																																			
DAY																																			
DATE																																			
THE STORE	A	B	C	D	E	A	B	C	D	E	A	B	C	D	E	A	B	C	D	E	A	B	C	D	E	A	B	C	D	E	A	B	C	D	E
GROCERY ITEMS																																			
DAIRY PRODUCTS																																			
1																																			
2																																			
LAUNDRY STUFF																																			
1																																			
2																																			
3																																			
PAPER PRODUCTS																																			
1																																			
2																																			
3																																			
DESSERTS																																			
1																																			
2																																			
3																																			
OTHER																																			
1																																			
2																																			
THE STORE	A	B	C	D	E	A	B	C	D	E	A	B	C	D	E	A	B	C	D	E	A	B	C	D	E	A	B	C	D	E	A	B	C	D	E

NAME ______________________ DATE ______________________

WEEK 3—IDENTIFICATION OF GROCERY STORES STUDIED—WEEK 3

A) ______________________ B) ______________________

C) ______________________ D) ______________________

E) ______________________

28 DAY COMPARATIVE GROCERY STORE EXERCISE																																			
DAY																																			
DATE																																			
THE STORE	A	B	C	D	E	A	B	C	D	E	A	B	C	D	E	A	B	C	D	E	A	B	C	D	E	A	B	C	D	E	A	B	C	D	E
GROCERY ITEMS																																			
BEVERAGE																																			
COFFEE																																			
TEA																																			
MILK																																			
CEREAL																																			
1																																			
2																																			
3																																			
FREEZER																																			
1																																			
2																																			
3																																			
FREEZER-MISC																																			
1																																			
2																																			
THE STORE	A	B	C	D	E	A	B	C	D	E	A	B	C	D	E	A	B	C	D	E	A	B	C	D	E	A	B	C	D	E	A	B	C	D	E

WEEK 3

SIDE 2—CONTINUED

28 DAY COMPARATIVE GROCERY STORE EXERCISE																																			
DAY																																			
DATE																																			
THE STORE	A	B	C	D	E	A	B	C	D	E	A	B	C	D	E	A	B	C	D	E	A	B	C	D	E	A	B	C	D	E	A	B	C	D	E
GROCERY ITEMS																																			
DAIRY PRODUCTS																																			
1																																			
2																																			
LAUNDRY STUFF																																			
1																																			
2																																			
3																																			
PAPER PRODUCTS																																			
1																																			
2																																			
3																																			
DESSERTS																																			
1																																			
2																																			
3																																			
OTHER																																			
1																																			
2																																			
THE STORE	A	B	C	D	E	A	B	C	D	E	A	B	C	D	E	A	B	C	D	E	A	B	C	D	E	A	B	C	D	E	A	B	C	D	E

NAME ______________________ DATE ______________________

WEEK 4—IDENTIFICATION OF GROCERY STORES STUDIED—WEEK 4

A) ______________________ B) ______________________

C) ______________________ D) ______________________

E) ______________________

28 DAY COMPARATIVE GROCERY STORE EXERCISE																																			
DAY																																			
DATE																																			
THE STORE	A	B	C	D	E	A	B	C	D	E	A	B	C	D	E	A	B	C	D	E	A	B	C	D	E	A	B	C	D	E	A	B	C	D	E
GROCERY ITEMS																																			
BEVERAGE																																			
COFFEE																																			
TEA																																			
MILK																																			
CEREAL																																			
1																																			
2																																			
3																																			
FREEZER																																			
1																																			
2																																			
3																																			
FREEZER-MISC																																			
1																																			
2																																			
THE STORE	A	B	C	D	E	A	B	C	D	E	A	B	C	D	E	A	B	C	D	E	A	B	C	D	E	A	B	C	D	E	A	B	C	D	E

WEEK 4

SIDE 2—CONTINUED

28 DAY COMPARATIVE GROCERY STORE EXERCISE																																			
DAY																																			
DATE																																			
THE STORE	A	B	C	D	E	A	B	C	D	E	A	B	C	D	E	A	B	C	D	E	A	B	C	D	E	A	B	C	D	E	A	B	C	D	E
GROCERY ITEMS																																			
DAIRY PRODUCTS																																			
1																																			
2																																			
LAUNDRY STUFF																																			
1																																			
2																																			
3																																			
PAPER PRODUCTS																																			
1																																			
2																																			
3																																			
DESSERTS																																			
1																																			
2																																			
3																																			
OTHER																																			
1																																			
2																																			
THE STORE	A	B	C	D	E	A	B	C	D	E	A	B	C	D	E	A	B	C	D	E	A	B	C	D	E	A	B	C	D	E	A	B	C	D	E

And, of course, watch for sales, but again be exceedingly cautious. For a store to declare a sale it only has to have a few items "on sale." The sale items, if you need them, are probably a great buy. If you can use a coupon with the sale item, it can amount to an even greater savings. Remember, though, that the purpose of the sale from the store manager's point of view is to get you into the store. *Watch the non-sale items.* Often, I have seen the prices on the non-sale items raised from two to five percent to make up for the loss being taken on the sale items. So, what you saved on buying the sale item, you quickly lost on purchasing the non-sale item. My suggestion is to use your shopping list. Buy only those identified sale items on your list and then leave the store.

As you might suspect, I pride myself on rarely going to the store without a coupon or purchasing goods on sale. In fact, I have saved as much as 20% each month just by using coupons alone. Combining couponing with shopping at the right store at the right time has been a boon to my financial plan! If my family's grocery bill is between $400 and $500 per month, my cost can be reduced to between $180 and $225 per month by carefully checking store prices and couponing.

Think about how much ***your*** grocery bill could be reduced each month just by knowing which market is the least expensive and on which day and by using coupons. Becoming a wise shopper is another way to find hidden money and begin managing your finances.

Credit Cards. Are you aware that the banks/credit card companies have your name and address already in their files? Are you aware that they waited for your high school graduation or your start of college to send you one of their credit cards? They needed some excuse to entice you to "charge."

In concept, there is nothing wrong with having a charge account or a credit card—provided you can keep it under control. However, many students find that having such a card can be a nightmare for them and can negatively impact their credit rating for the next ten years, if not for the rest of their lives.

If possible, don't charge items. Avoid using plastic if you can. Plastic costs money. Many credit cards today are charging 18 - 21% per year in interest. This is money out of your pocket. A credit card balance of $1000 costs you an additional $180 to $210 each year if a balance remains on the card. Defer immediate gratification and wait until you can pay with cash. Think of what you could do with that extra $180-$210!

The secret to using plastic is to pay your card off entirely each month. What?!? That's right. Avoid leaving a balance on your credit card account. By having a balance you are paying interest on the interest that they are charging you for the privilege to use their card.

Therefore, if you must charge, make sure you can pay the entire credit card off in one or two payments. Otherwise, my suggestion is: Don't charge at all. Instead, wait until you have the cash.

Roper College Track estimates that almost three million college students own credit cards. For many credit is a useful tool, but for some, it can get them dangerously in debt. Richard Vega, in his article entitled "Money," (December 1-3, 1995, *USA Weekend Edition*) reported that a 1994 study of Mississippi college seniors showed that the majority of the students studied kept pace with their credit cards. However, the study also showed that a growing percentage of students are "in over their heads." In fact, one student in the research study had more than 20 different credit cards!

Let me make my point by telling you about two students I know. Rich K. was an average student who graduated from the local high school in the middle of his class with average grades. He was planning to attend the local community college. A month before his high school graduation he received an *unrequested* credit card with a credit line of $1,500. All he had to do was sign the card enclosed and mail it back in the self-addressed, postage-paid envelope. Easy. He signed it. By the end of June, only three weeks after his graduation, he had charged over $1,200 on this card. Rich K.'s summer job gave him take-home funds (after deductions) of around $108 per week. Doesn't sound bad, but Rich K. will soon find out exactly how expensive a 19.9% interest charge per year can be each month.

My second case is Jamie S. Jamie graduated with high honors from her high school. She had a full scholarship to an ivy league university. From the summer of her graduation until she began at the university Jamie received not one unrequested credit card, but ***twelve***. Each card had a credit line of from $2,500 to $5,000. Jamie S. was unemployed. She had no summer job and no plans for one. Instead, Jamie took two college courses at the local community college to earn some advanced standing credit at the university. Also, at the university she did not plan to work. It was expected that the scholarship would provide for her needs and expenses. Wrong. By the end of the second month of Jamie's first semester, she was more than $35,000 in debt to eight of the twelve credit card companies.

As further reported by Vega in his "Money" article, "Credit card issuers targeted students after the market became saturated less than a decade ago. From their standpoint, it is a sound strategy: New customers arrive on campus each semester, 67 percent of cardholders stick with their first card, and statistically, credit companies say, students remain less of a credit risk than the general adult population." However, if this continues to be a practice, these companies will continue to send out their credit cards to persons like Rich and Jamie who consider the credit cards to be a ticket to "free money." Teenagers and adults alike need to begin looking at credit cards as providing easy access to "loan" funds and not convince themselves that the items they are charging are a gift.
What happened to Rich K. and Jamie S.? Because Rich continued his job, part-time, while he attended the local community college, he found it possible to make his payments. However, after one year of not using the card and having monthly interest added onto the principal, he still owed almost $1,000.

Jamie, on the other hand, did not have as much luck. She was forced to withdraw from the university and get a job. However, without a college degree she could only get minimum wage jobs. At the end of one year she was forced to file for bankruptcy. This one move will likely have a negative impact on her credit for the rest of her life. On the brighter side, Jamie is now back at the local college part-time and working full-time. She realizes that for her a credit card is addicting. When she gets one in the mail, she cuts it up.

Perhaps you are having a hard time believing these stories. "This will never happen to me," you might be thinking. Unfortunately, if the trend continues, you, too could be a victim of too many credit cards and too much credit. In fact, the April, 1996 issue of ***Money Magazine*** (p. 161) reported: ". . .that people at all income levels are overextended."

Credit cards under control are a luxury. However, credit cards, like a drug, can be addictive and can be abused. When abused, they can be very destructive for one's future. Be careful with how you borrow and use credit.

Sources of Financial Aid

Earlier, I indicated that one of your best investments is a college education. One thing I did not mention was how your education was to be paid for. If you have honor grades, you may be able to get a scholarship to attend many four-year colleges and universities. Perhaps you have athletic talent or musical ability or another skill which makes you a particularly attractive candidate to some institutions. In that case, you may be granted a "free ride." But what is out there for those who do not have extraordinary grades or sought-after talents?

Local, state and federal money is available for attending any and all levels of higher education. Did you know that? The amount of money available is approaching ***ten billion dollars***. Amazingly, almost half of it does not get used because students do not apply for it. Below, I will give you the most popular financial funds and programs. Others also exist. All you need to do to find out about them is contact your local community college, college or university and ask them for information. (You could be a postage stamp or phone call away from receiving anywhere from $500 each year to more than $2,500.)

Wouldn't this money make attending college a little easier? Most financial aid could reduce your college costs by 30 to 60 percent. Isn't it worth the effort and study to investigate what is available for you?

Finding money for college can be easy. Before the arrival of the modem and computer the traditional way was to check with your local high school, community college, college and university for addresses to which to apply. If you have access to a computer with a modem, all you need to do is dial the following World Wide Web numbers:

<http://www.ed.gov> or
<www.ed.gov/prog_info/ SFA/StudentGuide/>

If you do not have access to a computer then dial the Federal Student Aid Information Center at 1-(800) 4-FED-AID (1-800-433-3243). Loan information is also available through **Educaid**. Educaid has student loan specialists available by calling 1-(800) EDUCAID (1-800-338-2243). Both these calls are free. So do not delay. Call them today and learn about funds that are available for your use.

Grants and Scholarships. The most common financial aid programs are grants and scholarships. These are aid awards that don't have to be repaid. However, some will require that you perform a service in exchange for the award. The recipient of a band scholarship, for example, may be required to devote a few nights a week to rehearsal and most of Saturday to playing his or her instrument at the college football games. It's a small price to pay for the chance to go to college.

Two of the more common grant programs are PELL and SEOG.

PELL. The Pell is a federally administered grant. It is unlike a loan in that it does not have to be repaid. Federal Pell Grants are awarded only to undergraduates who have not previously earned a bachelor's or professional degree. (A professional degree would be a degree such as law, or dentistry, or pharmacy.) For many students, Pell Grants provide much of the foundation money for their financial aid package. A recipient of a Pell Grant may have other aid awarded to them based upon need. Students may be awarded Federal Pell Grant money for less than full time attendance, although the award will be reduced. For more information on the dollar amount of awards given you'll need to contact your specific institution of planned attendance.

To determine financial aid eligibility requires each applicant to complete Student Aid Report (SAR). The U.S. Department of Education uses a standard formula, established by Congress, to evaluate the information you provide in your SAR. The formula produces an Expected Family Contribution (EFC) number. The EFC is subtracted from the Cost of Attendance (COA) and this produces a students financial need. The formula looks like this:

COA – EFC = FINANCIAL NEED.

For additional information regarding Federal Pell Grant money, you may call 1-800-433-3243 or write to Federal Student Aid Information, P.O. Box 84, Washington, DC 20044.

SEOG. Another popular grant program is the Federal Supplemental Educational Opportunity Grant. How do SEOG and PELL differ? The U.S. Department of Education guarantees that each participating school will receive enough money to pay Pell Grants to its eligible students. However, there is no guarantee that every eligible student can receive a SEOG, since these funds are based on availability. SEOG funds are intended for undergraduates with exceptional financial need; that is, students with the lowest Expected Family Contributions (EFCs). Students who receive a SEOG award also receive a Pell Grant. Neither of these grants needs to be paid back. The amount of a SEOG award can vary from as little as $100 to as much as $4,000 per year.
For more information regarding Federal Supplemental Education Opportunity Grants, you may call or write the Federal Student Aid Information office at the phone number or address above.

Loans are sums of money that must be repaid. To qualify as financial aid, loans must carry an interest rate that is lower than prevailing commercial rates. They must also offer favorable repayment provisions. For example, in the Stafford Loan Program, borrowers do not start paying interest on the loan nor do they have to retire any of the principal until nine months after completing their studies.

Work-Study is the third most popular financial aid program. Work-Study counts as financial aid when employment is arranged for you through your institutions financial aid office. Employment may be on- or off-campus. At many colleges, you are required to be a full-time student, if you accept work-study. (The exact credit hour requirement for full-time varies from campus to campus. Full-time attendance usually means a minimum of twelve semester hours or fifteen term hours.) The number of hours each week that you are permitted to work are also regulated. Usually students are permitted to work more than fifteen hours per week; however, under special circumstances, twenty-hour work weeks may be arranged. The program encourages community service work and work related to ones, course of study. For more information about financial aid, it is important that you contact the financial aid office at the college or university you plan to attend.

A final note: To receive financial aid in time for the beginning of a new semester will take planning on your part. You cannot leave this for the last minute. There are (application) to be completed and mailed out. It takes time. The financial aid office will need information from you. Some of this information must be notarized. In other words, if you are to use the abundant financial aid money that is available to you, don't expect to wait until the last minute to get it. Procrastination means you end up paying a greater portion of college cost than you need to.

CORNERSTONES FOR FINDING HIDDEN MONEY

CORNERSTONES

- Comparison shop
- Use coupons and shop for sale items
- Buy snack foods in bulk or cut down on them altogether
- Pay your credit card balance off in full each month
- Cut up any unsolicited credit cards which come to you in the mail.
- Before driving somewhere, call ahead to find out if what you are looking for is at your destination.
- Plan your driving trips carefully so you don't end up backtracking.
- Keep your spending to a minimum by not carrying too much cash, a debit card or a credit card.
- When you shop, keep receipts and watch for errors on your billing statements. When you find them, notify the biller and request a refund.
- Fix things yourself when they break—or better yet, before they break.
- Include "fun" things in your budget, but avoid overspending.
- When you create a budget, stick to it.

ONE MINUTE JOURNAL EXERCISE

A) In 30 seconds or less, jot down three major ideas you learned from this section.

____

____

____

____

____

B) In 30 seconds or less, jot down how you see yourself applying these ideas

____

____

____

____

____

BUILDING A FINANCIAL PLAN

In the "At This Moment. . ." exercise earlier in this chapter, you determined how you think about money. Regardless of your answers, there is only one thing that remains consistent: **money is necessary to meet your current and future economic needs.**

Finding financial independence requires you to plan.

You're probably wondering where some people seemed to have learned certain "secrets" for obtaining great amounts of money. Truthfully, the "secrets" may be easier than you think. One strategy is *planning*. I will keep repeating this.

Another strategy is to *save and invest the dollars you earn today for tomorrow.* Following these two strategies is the essence of financial planning. Financial planning allows you to take control of your finances. "Yeah," you may be saying, "But I'm just a college student—I'm too young to think about financial planning. I barely have the money to buy a new pair of running shoes." Financial planning is for everyone—including college students. You need to start managing your money while you are still in school and forming (or modifying) your spending habits. Once you make a habit of taking charge of your finances it will become a major factor in creating a more satisfying life for you. Remember, planning today for tomorrow is the only way to free yourself from money concerns in the future.

The first step—indeed, the *key*—to financial planning is to assess where you are now and where you want to go. Once you have set your goals you then have an idea of how much money you need to achieve them. Every successful business — big and small — has a financial plan (a budget) so it can get the most out of each dollar. Consider your life and your money as if you were running a small business. Recognize now that to be successful will require you to plan carefully.

ASSESSING YOUR FINANCIAL POSITION

To have a successful financial plan requires you to know your financial situation. What are your **assets** (what you own), your current **debts** (what you owe), your needs, future expenses and budget? Take a minute to figure out your financial condition. Use the following chart adapted from ***The Money Book of Personal Finance*** to compute your current debt status.

CURRENT DEBT STATUS

Loans and charge accounts: Not listed are first mortgages or credit cards paid in full each month.

Last Month's Payments

______________________	$ ________
______________________	$ ________
______________________	$ ________
______________________	$ ________
______________________	$ ________
______________________	$ ________
______________________	$ ________
______________________	$ ________
______________________	$ ________
______________________	$ ________

1. **Last month's total payments** $ ________

2. **Monthly after-tax income** $ ________

3. **Your debt-to-income ratio** $ ________
   Divide line 1 by line 2. This is the percentage of your take-home pay that goes to pay your non-mortgage debt.
4. **See the table below to determine if you have too much debt.**

If your age is ______ **and line 3 is** ______

	0-10%	10-15%	15-20%	20%+
Under 35	A	A	B	C
35-55 (one wage-earner in household)	A	B	C	C
35-55 (two wage-earners in household)	A	A	B	C
Over 55	A	B	C	C

Code Explanation:
A = You are doing fine.
B = Watch it.
C = You are in trouble.

Good. You completed the debt exercise. Do you have too much debt?

What can you do about the situation? We talked earlier about taking control of credit cards so you have more money for savings and investments. Remember, when you must borrow, borrow creatively and carefully.

Okay, so now you are aware of your current financial debt. What about your assets? How much are you actually worth? Below is an Asset and Liabilities Balance Sheet. Calculate your liabilities and assets. The difference is your **net worth**.

ASSET AND LIABILITIES BALANCE SHEET
as of ____________ (date)

Assets	Liabilities
Real Estate	Mortgages
Personal Property	Taxes
Autos	Operating Expenses
Accounts Receivable	Accounts Payable
Cash	Insurance Premiums
Savings	Loans (payments due others)
Checking	Installments
Time Deposits	Store Charge Accounts
Stocks	Bank Credit Cards
Mutual Funds	Other Liabilities
Bonds	
Government Bonds	
Pension	
Annuity	
Profit-Sharing	
Cash-Value Life Insurance	
Loans (Payments Receivable)	
Other Assets	
TOTAL ASSETS	TOTAL LIABILITIES
	Total Assets
	LESS Total Liabilities
	NET WORTH

Is your net worth positive or negative? If your net worth is positive, that is terrific! You can begin now to plan to set aside a small portion of your money for long term investment. You can actually save. On the other hand, if your net worth is negative, then much work needs to be done. You need to develop a financial plan to get your net worth to the plus side. This will require you to develop and keep a household budget.

Budgeting is really planning. Watching and calculating how much money is coming in each month and how much you spend is important to taking control of your finances. While not having control of your income and expenditures may not be a problem this week or next, it is sure to become one soon if the money you are spending each month exceeds the money coming in!

Carefully map out a monthly household operating budget as well as a college semester/term budget. This will give you a better picture of your expenses each month. The Estimated Budget of Resources/Income, the Estimated College Semester/Term Expense Budget and the Estimated Monthly Household Operating Budget forms on the next few pages will help you. Remember to make multiple copies of these forms so you can update and recalculate your budget.

A word of advice: Clearly identify where the money is coming from and where it is being spent. Some of the more usual **fixed expenses** (expenses which remain the same each month) during the year include: mortgage/rent, insurance premiums, loans, and school tuition. **Variable** or **flexible expenses** (expenses which vary in amount paid each month) include: utilities, home repairs, medical/dental, magazines/newspapers, groceries, auto expenses, textbooks, clothing, entertainment, and other miscellaneous items. **When possible, make savings a fixed expense. If your net worth is on the negative side, then give up the savings until your net worth is positive.**

It is important that you carefully list all fixed and flexible expenses. Accuracy is essential here.

ESTIMATED BUDGET OF RESOURCES/INCOME
prepared as of __________(date)

SOURCE	ESTIMATED AMOUNT
Work-Self (full-time)	$ __________
Work-Self (part-time)	$ __________
Spouse Income	$ __________
Parental Contribution	$ __________
Savings	$ __________
Loans	$ __________
Investments	$ __________
Other	$ __________

EXERCISE

What have you learned from this exercise?

How do you feel about it?

ESTIMATED COLLEGE SEMESTER/TERM EXPENSE BUDGET
prepared as of ______________ (date)

EXPENSE ITEM	ESTIMATED COST Monthly	Yearly
Tuition	$ __________	$
Books and supplies	$ __________	$
Housing	$ __________	$
Utilities	$ __________	$
Phone	$ __________	$
Transportation	$ __________	$
Clothing	$ __________	$
Food	$ __________	$
Household Items	$ __________	$
Laundry	$ __________	$
Health Care	$ __________	$
Recreation/fun	$ __________	$
Miscellaneous	$ __________	$

ESTIMATED MONTHLY HOUSEHOLD OPERATING BUDGET
prepared as of __________ (date) for ________________

		Jan.	Feb.	March	April	May	June	July	Aug.	Sept.	Oct.	Nov.	Dec.	Total
	Total Income													
Fixed Payments	*Mortgage (rent)*													
	Taxes													
	Insurance													
	Loans (Payments due to others)													
	Savings													
	Total Fixed Payments													
Flexible Payments	*Utilities*													
	House Improvements/Repairs													
	Food													
	Clothing													
	Medical/Dental													
	Education													
	Recreation													
	Magazines/Newspapers													
	Contributions													
	Automobile Expenditures													
	Credit Charges													
	Other													
	Total Flexible Payments													
Budget	*Total Fixed and Flexible*													
	Total Income													
	Balance (+ or –)													

ONE MINUTE JOURNAL EXERCISE

A) In 30 seconds or less, jot down three major ideas you learned from this section.

____

____

____

____

____

____

B) In 30 seconds or less, jot down how you see yourself applying these ideas.

____

____

____

____

____

____

PLANNING FOR YOUR FINANCIAL SUCCESS

Most people will not work forever. According to the Bureau of Labor Statistics, the average male in a blue collar job works approximately 40 years; the average single female in a blue collar job works approximately 43 years; and the married female in the same job works 25 to 30 years. For those in white collar jobs, males work between 30 and 35 years and females work between 25 to 30 years.

Let us assume, for example purposes, that you work until you are 65. If you took good care of yourself and did not engage in high risk activity, we'll assume that you could live to 85 years of age or older. How do you expect to support yourself in your latter 20 or even 30 years of life while you are not working? If married, how would you support yourself and your family? While the common assumption is that children will be grown and living on their own by the time you retire, that isn't always true for many of today's families. Since the 1970's, a growing number of men and women have had first families and second families well into their forties and their fifties. In addition, there is also a rise in the number of grandparents rearing their grandchildren. It is now quite possible that children will still be at home and getting ready to attend college when you are planning to call it quits from work and retire. How will the necessary expenses be met?

The secret is planning.

Where will the necessary money come from during those years that you are not working or are not able to work? It is in preparation for these years that financial planning and investment comes in particularly handy. Make a plan to save and invest your dollars earned today to free yourself from money concerns in the future.

BEING EDUCATED ABOUT INVESTING: THE RULE OF 72.

Part of effective financial planning is knowing the **Rule of 72**. The Rule of 72 is a quick-and- easy way to estimate how long it will take an investment to double your money. The calculation goes as follows:

Divide 72 by the annual return expected.

For example, if an investment has a 10% annual yield (return), divide 72 by 10 and you will get 7.2 as your answer [72/10 = 7.2]. Thus, 7.2 is the number of years it will take your money to double with that 10% return. Here is another example: At 9%, it takes about 8 years for your money to double [72/9 = 8]. You do a couple.

EXERCISE

You were very fortunate and found an investment paying a 12% annual yield. Using the Rule of 72, how long will it take for your investment money to double? In the space below, show how you arrived at your answer.

The answer is: ______________________________

In 1985, you put $1000 into an investment fund. For the past 12 years this fund has paid an annual interest yield of 12%. You allowed your money and interest to compound. To the nearest $100, what is your investment worth 12 years later? In the space below, show how you calculated your answer.

The answer is: ______________________________

Who says word problems aren't fun!??

Remember, when it comes to investing, time is of the essence. It is important that you begin today to plan for your financial security tomorrow.

EXERCISE

Do you now understand the rule of 72? How can you use it in your life?

____

____

____

____

____

____

____

REASONS WHY FINANCIAL PLANS FAIL

Procrastination. Many people keep putting off their financial planning. They tell themselves that they will do it next week, next year, or after they graduate or when they pay off their car. Others say they are not ready or they do not have the money now. Still others tell me that "I am only 18 or 20 or 25 or 45." Stop making excuses. **This book is based on action; not excuses.** You need to take action today. People who invest regularly, do not procrastinate. They know the secret of **compound interest**. Look at the chart below.

$100 CONTRIBUTED MONTHLY INTO TAX DEFERRED INVESTMENT FUNDS AT DIFFERENT RATES OF INTEREST AND ALLOWING TO COMPOUND FOR 5 TO 30 YEARS

Percentage Rate	5 Years	10 Years	20 Years	30 Years
3	6,474	13,979	32,766	58,014
4	6,652	14,774	36,800	69,636
5	6,829	15,593	41,275	83,573
6	7,012	16,470	46,435	100,954
7	7,201	17,409	52,295	122,709
8	7,397	18,417	59,295	150,030
9	7,599	19,497	67,290	184,447
10	7,808	20,655	76,570	227,933
11	8,025	21,899	87,357	283,023
12	8,249	23,234	99,915	352,991
13	8,480	24,668	114,552	442,706
14	8,720	26,209	131,635	555,706
15	8,968	27,866	151,595	700,982

SOURCE: Adapted, from compound interest and annuity charts provided from TIAA-CREF compounding interest calculator-1995, T. Rowe Price compounding interest retirement savings calculator-1995, and successful money Management Seminar-1995

Isn't it amazing what tax deferred money and interest compounded for over 30 years can produce? Can you imagine what would happen if you let that money continue to grow for 40 years?

Look again at the chart. Would you believe that as little as $3.33 per day invested in a fund paying an annual yield of 12% will produce more than $300,000 in 30 years and over one million dollars in only 40? It does not sound like much when you say $3,33 per day, but that comes to $100 per month. Are you surprised at how little money you need to make your financial goal come true? It is possible that you and your family may be wasting this amount of money each month? Go back to the section on snacking earlier in this chapter. Are you wasting $3.33 each day?

EXERCISE

In the next section list all the ways you can think that you and your family wastes money. Be honest. Your future financial security depends upon it.

Begin now to avoid procrastination.

In the mid-nineteen forties and fifties it was a common practice for parents to buy an insurance policy called "an endowment" for their child or children. The price was rather inexpensive. The average policy for $10,000 was around $160 per year or only $13.33 per month. The idea was that it would grow in value to $10,000 in 21 years. When the child reached 21 or 22 his or her parents gave him or her a gift for a new hous, college, or to start their own "nest egg."

Let us assume, for discussion purposes, that you put away for yourself (each of your children) the amount of $13.33 monthly in a fund paying 12%. This is only $160 per year. According to Estes and Kelley, authors of McGraw-Hill's *Compound Interest & Annuity Tables*, if you leave this money alone for 21 years and allow it to compound interest, it will produce a fund of more than $40,000! Remember those insurance companies offered to pay your children $10,000 for your $160 investment. Clearly, this was a very good deal for insurance companies. If $160 is not difficult for you to deposit into a 12% mutual fund on a yearly basis, then do it. After 21 years, you (or your children) will have $40,000 if you wait another 30 to 40 years, this investment will produce a retirement fund of more than **$2,000,000**!

Think about this for a moment. Is $13.33 per month too much to invest in your child's future? or your own? This is only $160 per year.

Stop procrastinating. Begin NOW to make your financial plan come true. Swallow the excuses. You may never be ready or it may never be the right time. Accept the fact that the right time is now. Take action.

EXERCISE

What have you learned from the above regarding and investing?

What do you plan to do about this observation?

LACK OF A "WINNING ATTITUDE".

Developing an effective financial plan takes effort, study, work, persistence and patience. If your plan encompasses a spouse, children or other extended family, it also requires that the family work together as a team. Each member of the team must be committed, disciplined, positive and willing to make some sacrifices to make the plan work. Like any goal, the goals for a financial plan must be realistic, attainable and measurable.

Unfortunately, many people today want immediate gratification. They want, as the expression goes, 'to have their cake and eat it too'. All too often, people refuse to acknowledge the work that goes into making a serious financial commitment. They refuse to put in the effort, study, work, persistence and patience it takes to make a financial plan become a reality. Instead of having a 'wanna' they may be experiencing the fear that can come from the thought of investing money. To be successful financially will require an individual to 'risk'. Many people today have fears about risking their hard-earned money. Often people are more willing to take a dollar and put it on a lottery ticket, rather than taking $100 or $1000 and putting it in a stock or mutual fund.
Are you aware that some of most successful people in the U.S. failed and then came back? They were willing to risk. According Patricia Sellers, in the May 1, 1995 issue of FORTUNE (v131 n8 p.48-58) "Failure. Personal, humiliating, image- wrecking failure is not as bad as you think. Richard Miller, the chief financial officer of AT&T, Anne Busquet, the highest-ranking female line manager at American Express, and Bernard Marcus, the founder and CEO of Home Depot, are just some of the big names who have screwed up, misstepped, gotten fired, been demoted, or in some other way failed spectacularly." Each experienced failure and came back. Each had a winning attitude.

I am proud to know "Rudy" and call him a friend. A movie was made called, surprisingly enough about him "Rudy" When Daniel "Rudy" E. Ruettiger was a kid, he had a dream. His dream was to graduate from Notre Dame and play football for the "fighting Irish." Rudy was only 5'6" tall and graduated third from the bottom of his class. This did not deter him.

Rudy was initially rejected from Notre Dame. But, he did not let this rejection stop him. He picked himself up, dusted himself off and attended nearby community college. Every semester, while at community college, he reapplied to Notre Dame. Each time he received a rejection letter he worked harder on his grades at the community college. Rudy pushed himself so hard at the community college that he made honors each semester. As a result, in his last semester of community college, he was accepted to Notre Dame.

Once at Notre Dame he had to work to make his dream come true: He was going to play for the Fighting Irish. Remember, in addition to Rudy's initial difficulty with learning, he was only 5'6" tall. Clearly, he was not your typical football player.

Rudy had "wanna." More than anything he wanted to make the team. He was willing to risk everything. With his enthusiasm, his drive, and his perseverance, he took the obstacles in front of him and made them into success steps. In his entire Notre Dame football career Rudy made only one tackle and played in only one game. Nevertheless, what he did to make and stay on that team was magnificent. He so inspired his teammates that at the end of the last game they carried him out on their shoulders to the shouts of the stadium crowd: "Ru-dy," "Ru-dy," "Ru-dy."

When a loser is knocked down, they stay there. A winner gets up.

As Rudy has shared with me, the difference between a winner and a loser is easy to understand.

Yes, these individuals above know what it is like to fail. They also know what it is like to achieve success and even greatness.

EXERCISE

Please answer the questions below

Do you know of someone who risked and lost? Yes ______ No ______

What were the consequences?

____

____

____

____

____

____

Is or was there something they could have done differently to prevent their failure?

____

____

____

____

____

____

Do you know someone who risked and made it? Yes ______ No ______

What were the consequences?

____

____

____

____

____

Do you want to have financial security? Yes ______ No ______

What will be the consequences of you not achieving it?

____

____

____

____

____

What will be the consequences of you achieving it?

____

____

____

____

____

Do the consequences of failing at achieving financial security outweigh the possibility of making it? As Rudy so clearly pointed out, **the difference between those who are successful and those who fail is that those who succeed know how to pick themselves up**. Are you aware **that for many the only deterrent to making money is the fear of losing it**? You can be a loser, but it is much more fun to be a winner.

EXERCISE

What can you do to give yourself the winner attitude?

____

____

____

____

____

Let's look at another reason why financial plans fail.

UNREALISTIC EXPECTATIONS.

In the past, many people said "I don't need a retirement plan, I can live off of social security." As you undoubtedly know from listening to the news, this thinking is unrealistic at best; disastrous at worst. According to the Bureau of Labor Statistics, in 1994 many men in America had total yearly incomes—including social security benefits—of approximately $14,500, and women fared even more poorly at annual incomes of $8,200. Full social security benefits (waiting to 65 years of age or beyond) will pay a maximum monthly allocation of approximately $1,200 for a male and $950 for a female. If the recipient has a non-working spouse, s/he is entitled to another $600—bringing the maximum monthly total to approximately $1,800 for a male and $1,550 for a female. These figures would give you an annual income of $21,600 and $18,500, respectively. Note, however, that most social security recipients do not receive maximum awards. Indeed, the average benefit paid is approximately $700 with an additional fifty percent ($350) for a non-working spouse. It saddens me to report that this is at or pretty close to the poverty level. And by the time you retire, will the Social Security Administration be able to fund even that level of annual income? What then? Clearly, social security alone will not provide for your future.

ONE MINUTE JOURNAL EXERCISE

A) In 30 seconds or less, jot down three major ideas you learned from this section.

____

____

____

____

____

____

B) In 30 seconds or less, jot down how you see yourself applying these ideas.

____

____

____

____

____

____

____

BECOMING A SMART INVESTOR:
KNOWING WHAT IS OUT THERE

Learning good habits of budgeting, planning and saving will pay dividends throughout your life. *You can even save if you make very little money.* I've said it before. Put away only $3.33 per day (that is, $100 per month) and invest it monthly in a fund paying 10% or more in annual interest, and after 40 years it will be worth more than $500,000. So, budget your savings the same way that you budget for food, tuition and other expenses. Always **pay yourself first**. Initially, put this money into a savings account until you have saved enough to open a longer-term, higher interest paying fund.

From time to time students have asked me questions like the following:
Are banks a good place to put my money?
Should I start a Christmas Club account?
Is a CD a good place for my money?
How about putting my money into stock?
Should I consider investing in a mutual fund?

The answer to these and other financial questions are both "yes" and "no." How you invest, what you select to invest in, and when you invest all depend on your financial plan, the life style you are currently living and the life style you wish to live in the future. No one can specifically answer the above questions for you. Each represent decisions you must explore and consider. However, the following exercise may give you some insight.

EXERCISE

Return to the chart on pp. 28 and answer the following questions.

If you want to make the greatest return of your investment in next thirty years, where should you put your money? (Remember the *Rule of 72*.)

1. In a saving account paying around 3%. If you put your $1200 each year into a savings account for the next 30 years your return, according to the chart on page **28** would be _________.
2. What would happen if you put your money into a bank money market? The interest rate return on a bank money market would be around 5%. If you put your $1200 into a money market and let it grow for the next 30, according to the chart on pp **28** you would have an investment fund worth __________.
3. You have heard a great deal about CDs (Certificates of Deposit). The return on a CD depends on how long you keep it (you actually state the length of time when you buy them) and the cash amount you are ready to invest. Let us assume for analysis purposes that you will put your $1200 into a CD, each year, for the next 30 years. Assuming you can secure a 6% rate of return, what would your CD portfolio be worth in 30 years? __________
4. A friend of yours tells you that you can make big bucks from investing in mutual funds and stocks. He tells you to take your $1200 each year and stick it into a variety of stocks and mutual funds. Although your friend is not a financial advisor, the two of you carefully study the market and your mutual fund options. After many months of study the two of you recognize the risks involved but are equally excited about making your selections. You invest in stock and mutual funds for 30 years. You have picked wisely and your investments are paying an average yearly return of 15%. Assuming that you put the entire $1200 each year into these funds, what would be the value of your investments after 30 years of making contributions? __________

Based upon the above exercises, if you were asked the following question, how would you respond? QUESTION: I am going to have $1200 a year to invest. I want the greatest return on my investment. I can handle risk. Should I put my money into savings, bank money markets, CDs, or stocks and mutual funds? Using information derived from the chart on pp **28**, what would be your answer?

____

____

____

____

____

____

Most people do not make investment decisions in a vacuum. Sound investing involves much time and knowledge. Any investment can be risky. Don't listen to friends and relatives who tell you about a "sure thing." There's no such thing as a "sure thing." Beware of those individuals who encourage you to consider quick money schemes. Remember, if you are really serious about investing, recognize that it will take effort, focus, study, work, persistence and patience.

CHOOSING A FINANCIAL PLANNER

Instead of listening to family and friends for the "hot tip," get a professional financial planner's advice and help. There are many good ones in your community seeking your business. However, be careful when selecting a financial advisor. Note the following Cornerstones for seeking financial help.

CORNERSTONES FOR FINDING HIDDEN MONEY

- Check them out completely
- Get references
- Keep in mind that good manners do not indicate personal integrity
- If the individual begins to engage in high-pressure tactics, say ""No."
- Be extremely cautious' especially if you are overwhelmed by jargon
- Ask financial advisors to explain their portfolio completely
- Do not allow anyone to prey on your fears
- If you are an older citizen use extreme caution
- Quickly report any investment fraud or abuse, despite any embarrassment or fear you may feel
- Be clear on the procedure for retrieving your principal or cashing out profits.
- When in doubt, check with your college or university for recommendations.

  It is quite possible that the institution you are attending teaches seminars in personal money management through their college of continuing education. Often times these teachers will be willing to answer simple questions and provide you direction for selecting a financial advisor. Please do *not* expect this person to become your financial advisor.
- Arrange to pay the planner a set fee for advice, not to invest your money for you until you are comfortable with their investment strategies.

Before seeking out a financial planner, I suggest that you become familiar with the different investment opportunities and funds available to you. In the pages that follow, I will briefly describe a variety of funds you might consider for investment.

STOCK AND BOND MUTUAL FUNDS.

The safest and most convenient option for beginners are stock and bond mutual funds. Investing in stocks and bonds directly is difficult due to the large amount of up-front money required, the sophistication of market timing and the vast amount of information necessary to make the right choices. In addition, investing directly in stocks and bonds requires a broker to buy them and the commissions you pay them may eat up your profits. Therefore, investing in individual stocks and bonds is generally unwise for beginners. Of course, as your assets grow, this may change and you might consider such an investment for your money later. Right now, stick with mutual funds.

A **mutual fund** is a pool of stocks, bonds or money-market securities (for example, short-term debt obligations such as Treasury Bills) that its managers acquire to earn its investors the best possible return. You invest in a mutual fund by purchasing shares. This makes you a part-owner -- along with thousands of others -- of the pool of securities the fund manager has assembled. Your holding entitles you to a proportionate share of the fund's earnings.

WHY INVEST IN MUTUAL FUNDS?

There are a number of excellent reasons to invest in mutual funds. First, mutual funds have full-time professional managers selecting securities and monitoring them 24 hours a day. Secondly, a mutual fund also gives you the kind of diversification—often in hundreds of different stock and bond issues -- that most of us couldn't afford as an independent investor. Should one or two of your stocks drop, the rest of the fund's holdings will cushion any loss and protect your overall investment. Finally, to invest in mutual funds requires only a modest amount of money. Most require a minimum investment of $1,000; some have minimums of $250 and $500; and others have no minimum at all. Do you see how it is possible to invest $25 per week (that is, $100 per month) in funds that have a potential to earn you more than 10-15% a year? Recognize that you could eventually select to invest in five different funds—maybe two stocks, two bonds and one money market—and be as broadly diversified as a multimillionaire!

HOW MUCH RISK IS IN A MUTUAL FUND?

Unlike banks, mutual funds have no insurance, but custodial banks hold their securities. If the fund company collapses or one of its managers runs off to Brazil, generally, your holdings would be safe. This does not mean that your money is protected from loss. As stated earlier, whenever you invest, you expose yourself to some risk. Perhaps you remember that fateful day in October of 1987 when average stock fell almost 21 percent. It was scary for lots of big and small investors. However, market downs can actually be good for investors. If you remember, the market also rebounded and has since experienced some fantastic growth for its investors. The key to investing wisely is not to panic when your mutual funds begin to fall. Hang in there and they will usually turn around.

HOW DO I SELECT A MUTUAL FUND?

Which mutual fund to select is a problem for many new investors. There are more than 2,800 funds from which to select. As a new investor, you will likely find the selections overwhelming. Initially, you may want to choose a broad-based fund—to spread your risk among many securities. Later, as you build your assets, you can sample more aggressive funds.

Mutual fund earning is divided into three parts:

- dividends (interest) on securities that the fund owns;
- profits on securities the fund sells; and
- appreciation in fund shares.

Funds that emphasize income (dividends or interest) pay monthly returns, while those that aim for growth over time will pay either annually or semi-annually.

The riskier the investment, the higher the potential payoff.

The nearer you are to needing the money, the more conservative your investment should be.

Picking a fund or funds to invest in depends on your personality and your tolerance for risk and uncertainty. If you think that you will sweat buckets and stay up nights from seeing your fund losing 10 percent of its value in 10 weeks (I would), then perhaps an aggressive, volatile fund is not the best choice for you. Of course, if you choose a fund so conservative that you barely have to look at the newspaper to know the share price, you may as well stay with certificates of deposit. Generally, in fact, you may consider this observation as a rule of thumb: The riskier the investment, the higher the potential payoff.

Here is another rule of thumb: The nearer you are to needing the money, the more conservative your investment should be. On the other hand, if you are saving for something 20 years into the future, you can take some risks. If you lose some of the money, you will still have years to recover it and earn more.

GLOSSARY OF FUNDS.

One thing that drives most people crazy are the different names given to funds. Below you'll find a small glossary of fund terms. Hopefully, this will help you to understand some of the differences:

Type of fund	Definition
Aggressive-Growth	Buy "hot" stocks in the belief that they will go higher.
Growth Funds	Buy stocks that have not moved, but they believe they will.
Growth and Income	Buy stocks with the belief that high dividends are near.
Balanced Fund	Add bonds to its stock portfolio.
Equity-Income Fund	A stock fund that pays solid dividends.
Flexible Income	Combines stocks and bonds to give good pay-outs even when the market drops some.
Bond Funds	Put money into interest-bearing safe stuff.
International Funds	Hunts for stock abroad. Good to have some.
Sector Funds	Sink money into a single industry—gold, health care, utilities
CD/Treasuries	Issued by bank/treasury and guaranteed. Low interest rates.

Remember, you'll need to consider your goals, personality and temperament when deciding which funds are right for you. The following is generally true regarding the different fund selections:

Growth Sector and Aggressive Growth funds are suitable for investors who can hold shares for at least five years and who won't panic in a market downturn. These funds turn the best long-term performances, but are riskier than other funds.

Growth-and-income, equity-income, and balanced-income funds aim to provide steady income from dividends and interest. They are also for those who can leave money for five years or more, but are not comfortable with growth funds.

Flexible-income funds and bond funds are designed for someone who needs a steady cash stream now. However, they are not without their dangers. Funds with very high yields may be invested in the bonds of municipalities or companies with low credit ratings. A bond fund can also boost its yield by holding mostly bonds that will mature in 10 years or longer. This could prove to be problematic for a conservative investor. Remember, when interest rates rise, bond prices fall; therefore, the longer a bond's maturity, the farther the potential fall. So, if you are looking for security, stay with funds investing in bonds of credit-worthy institutions that mature in 2-5 years.

Lastly, the **global and international funds** may fall into any of the above three groups, depending on the kinds of securities in them. Beware that currency fluctuation can endanger your investment. Because the funds' investments are denominated in foreign currencies, the value of your holdings depends on the strength of the U.S. dollar relative to the foreign currencies. If the dollar is strong your return will be reduced because it will cost you more money to redeem your shares and switch them back to dollars.

HOW DO I GET MONEY OUT OF MY MUTUAL FUNDS?

You can claim appreciation in the price of your fund shares any time by redeeming them. Unless your mutual funds are lodged with tax-deferred savings plans [for example, Individual Retirement Accounts (IRA) or Keoghs], you will pay taxes on dividends and interest every year. Also, you will pay taxes on sales of securities or mutual fund shares in those years that you receive any income from them.

HOW MUCH SHOULD I EXPECT TO PAY FUND MANAGERS?

Your mutual funds make money for themselves by charging you fees. Many funds levy charges of 4.5 to 8.5% (the current law allows them to go as high as 9.9 percent) whenever you initially buy into a fund. Others charge no initial commission (or front-end load), but assess a back-end load when you sell shares—usually 1 to 5 percent of the amount you withdraw (but it can decrease to 0 for many funds held beyond six years and then sold). Others skim off a bit (called a 12b-1 fee) each year equal to 0.5 to 1.25 percent of your share of the fund's assets. Many funds charge all of the above. Don't worry. You want your fund managers to get paid so they continue to provide an excellent service for you.

CORNERSTONES FOR GOOD INVESTING

- The riskier the investment, the higher the potential payoff.
- The nearer you are to needing the money, the more conservative your investment should be.
- Do not buy a mutual fund until you have read its prospectus and understand its investment philosophy and objectives.
- Do not just pick top-rated funds. A fund at the top this month can be at the bottom next year. If you want safety for your investment, reject anything with a rating of less than "AA" by Standard and Poor's.
- Avoid any funds whose expenses exceed 1 percent of their assets.
- Consider service when selecting a fund. Does the management company offer you a variety of funds? Can you switch easily? Does the telephone representative offer help or do they laugh at your questions?

EXERCISE

Highlight those items from this section that you want to remember.

Developing a Winning Attitude:

Making Your Financial Plan Come True

To make your dreams and goals into a reality requires that you plan. As we've said before -- it takes effort, study, work, persistence and patience. However, things that you want are worth all of that. Don't let the time involved, past financial setbacks, previous disappointments or current financial mistakes or conditions knock you down.

Many potential financial winners quickly become losers because after being knocked down by misfortune they do not get up again. Remember: many of the most successful financial wizards have had financial setbacks. Yet they came back because they also had a focus and a dream.

In the *FORTUNE* article mentioned earlier, Sellers reported that Bill Gates, the president of Microsoft, is known for his regular attempts at failure. In fact, according to the author, Mr. Gates likes to hire people who know what it is to risk and to have failed. Sellers quotes Mr. Gates as saying: " The way people deal with things that go wrong is an indicator of how they deal with change." Mr. Gates wants people who risk and are willing to fail because he sees them as change agents.

In the July-August, 1995 issue of *SUCCESS*, special attention was paid to those who had made it then failed. The article "Great comebacks," by Michael Warshaw included the stories of ten entrepreneurs who fought their way back from financial defeat and disaster. Each subject had built a business success only to have it destroyed by poor planning, debilitating injury, theft, betrayal, or natural disaster. Each of them came back from despair to rebuild the old business or start a new one which is still thriving.

They learned from their disappointments and mistakes. You, too, can learn from your past financial mistakes and experiences. Pick yourself up, dust yourself off, and ask yourself "What can I do so that this financial catastrophe doesn't happen to me or my family again?"

There are still many more success stories which arise after failure. Sellers reports that "History is littered with heroes who failed. An ad agency reportedly fired Walt Disney for a 'singular lack of drawing ability,' and Disney went bankrupt with early ventures before making money bigtime. So did Henry Ford. So did Babe Ruth, who hit lots of home runs, and also broke the major league record for strikeouts: 1,330." These people and others certainly know what it is like to fail.

At the Harvard business school, professor John Kotter is quoted by Sellers as saying: "I can imagine a group of executives 20 years ago discussing a candidate for a top job and saying, 'This guy had a big failure when he was 32.' Everyone else would say, 'Yep, yep, that's a bad sign." I can imagine that same group considering a candidate today and saying,' "What worries me about this guy is that he's never failed.'."

Whether one wishes to face it or not, failure today is an asset. It's an indication of a willingness to try something new or different. Most of all its shows a willingness to risk. To make money one must be willing to risk. How much risk are you able to handle? Your answer may be an indication of exactly how conservative or aggressive you are willing to be in creating a financial plan.

Think of it. Your success now and in the future depends on what you do. Do you realize the power that you hold? You are in control. Knowing what you want gives you that power and control. State what you want clearly and exactly. Put this financial plan/goal into a written statement and tack it to your door, your medicine cabinet, the top of your desk. Keep it in front of you always. Take a few minutes and do the financial plan exercise that follows.

ONE MINUTE JOURNAL EXERCISE

A) In 30 seconds or less, jot down three major ideas you learned from this section.

____

____

____

____

____

B) In 30 seconds or less, jot down how you see yourself applying these ideas.

____

____

____

____

____

MAKING YOUR FINANCIAL PLAN COME TRUE

My financial plan/goal is to

____

____

____

State clearly when you want to have your plan/goal achieved. Give yourself a definite date and time that you plan to have it fulfilled.

I plan to have my financial plan/goal achieved on ______________ (day), ______________ (date) at ______________ (time).

Be honest with yourself. Begin to think about the cost and loss. Admit what the cost/the loss would be if you didn't achieve your financial goal.

For not obtaining my financial goal, I would experience the following costs and losses:

____

____

____

____

Can you accept these? YES______ NO______

Next, consider what gains may be in store for you for achieving your financial goal.

The gains that I would experience for achieving my financial goal are:

Don't the gains make the financial goal even more desirable? YES_______ NO_______

Begin at once to make your financial goal into a reality. Stop making excuses that you are not ready. Take action today. Remember, a journey of 1000 miles begins with a single step. Take that first step today.

Focus: Read your financial plan/goal statement aloud, twice daily -- once just before bed and once first thing in the morning. As you read and reread your goal statement, see and feel and believe yourself already in possession of the goal. Remember, what you think is how you feel. How you feel determines how you act. How you act controls what you become. Therefore, when you think it, plan it, you can achieve it, because you are in control.

CORNERSTONES FOR MONEY MANAGEMENT

- No more excuses; take action today!
- Make a budget and stick to it.
- Look for outside sources of financial aid.
- Beware the money enticers and look for sources of hidden money.
- Keep your financial plan/goal where you can see it and read it every day.
- Find places to put your savings where you earn no less than 10% or more each year.
- Make saving a habit.
- A college education is the best investment you can make.
- Begin today to plan for tomorrow.

EXERCISE

What have you learned from this section?

How do you feel about it?

FIVE MINUTE MONEY SUMMARY JOURNAL EXERCISE

A) In 2 minutes or less, jot down the three best ideas you learned from the previous ONE MINUTE JOURNAL EXERCISES.

B) In 2 minutes or less, jot down how you see yourself applying these ideas.

C) In 1 minute or less, jot down how you feel about what you learned?

REFERENCES

Belsky, Gary. How can you win your war against DEBT? *MONEY*, April, 1996, vol. 25, n 4, pg. 158-167.

Ellis, Junius (Ed.) *Money Advisor 1996.* NY, NY: Money Books, 1996.

Ellis, Junius, Alcorn, Ellen, and Fuller, Randy (Eds.) *MUTUAL FUNDS*: Winning Strategies for the 1990's. NY, NY: Money Magazine, 1993.

Estes, Jack C., and Kelley, Denis R. *McGraw-Hill's Compound Interest and Annuity Tables*, Second Edition. McGraw-Hill, Inc., 1993.

Fitzgerald, Randy. You Can Make a Million. *Readers Digest.* July 1996, p. 26.

Ferrett, Sharon K. *PEAK Performance.* Boston, MA: Irwin Mirror, 1994.

Goodman, Jordan E. and Block, Sonny. *Everyone's Money Book.* Chicago, IL: Dearborn Financial Publishing 1994.

Harris, Marlys (Ed.) *THE ESSENTIALS OF MONEY.* NY, NY: Money Magazine, 1994.

Sellers, Patricia. So you fail. Now bounce back. (How successful people recover from failures). *FORTUNE,* May 1, 1995, v131 n8 p.48-58.

Lynch, Peter. *LEARN TO EARN* NY, NY: Simon & Schuster, Inc., 1995.

Retirement Savings Calculator. Cincinnati, OH: T. Rowe Price, 1995.

Securities Division, 10 tips to avoid investment fraud, 1995 pamphlet.

Successful Money Management Seminar. U.S.A.: 1985-1995.

The Student Guide to Financial Aid, 1996-1997. U.S. Department of Education, 1995.

Understanding the Basics of Investing. Boston, MA: Fidelity Investments: Tax-Exempt Services Company, 1993.

U.S. News & World Report (Eds.) *The Complete FAMILY FINANCIAL RECORD BOOK.* Washington, D.C.: U.S. News/World Report, 1975.

Warshaw, Michael. Great comebacks. *SUCCESS.* July-Aug 1995, v42 n6 p33-46.

What is a MUTUAL FUND? Kansas City, MO: Twentieth Century, 1994.